Collins

1000
English
Words

Let's Get
Started
Activity Book

Rebecca Adlard
illustrated by Duc Nguyen

Contents

How to use this book

Hello!

In this book, there are lots of games and fun activities to help you practise English words.

Before you start, you can think about what words you know for each topic. You can make a word map and add new words from this book.

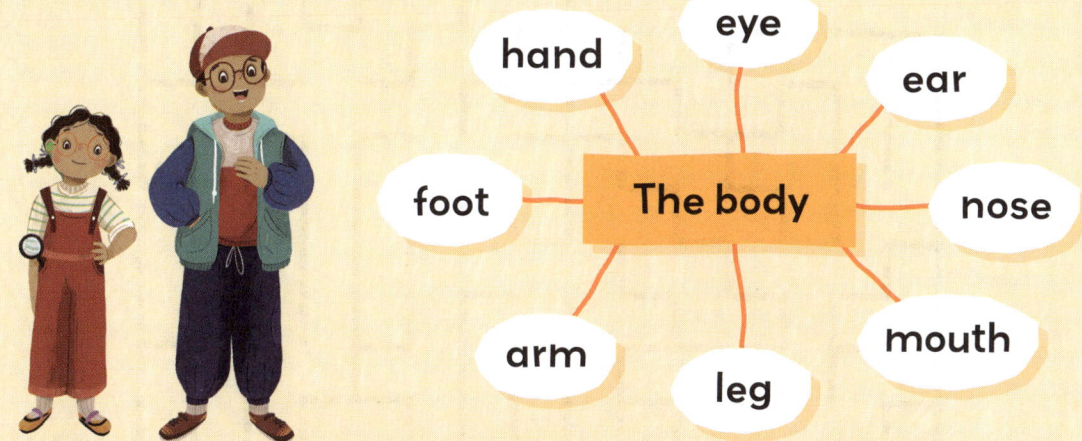

hand

eye

ear

foot

The body

nose

arm

leg

mouth

Oscar and Mia are here to help you. How many times can you find them in this book?

- When you see this ⭐, there's an extra activity from Oscar and Mia.

- When you see this ❓, you can learn an interesting fact. Tell your friends and family!

- When you see this 🖱, go to **collins.co.uk/eltresources** for extra fun.

- Use the word list on page 32 and tick ✓ all the words you learn!

And when you finish a game or activity, you can check your answers on pages 28–31.

All the words from this book can be found fully illustrated in *Collins 1000 English Words* visual dictionary.

You can go to **collins1000englishwords.com** to find a glossary with audio.

My family

Maze

Help Oscar and Mia get through the maze to Mum and Dad.

Let's draw! Go online to draw and write about you.

Word circles

Use each letter in the circle to make a family word. Start with the letter in the middle of the circle.

Wordmatch

Match the word parts to make five more family words.

cou	ter
sis	ma
grand	band
un	sin
brot	cle
hus	her

Pairs

Draw lines to match the people and make pairs.

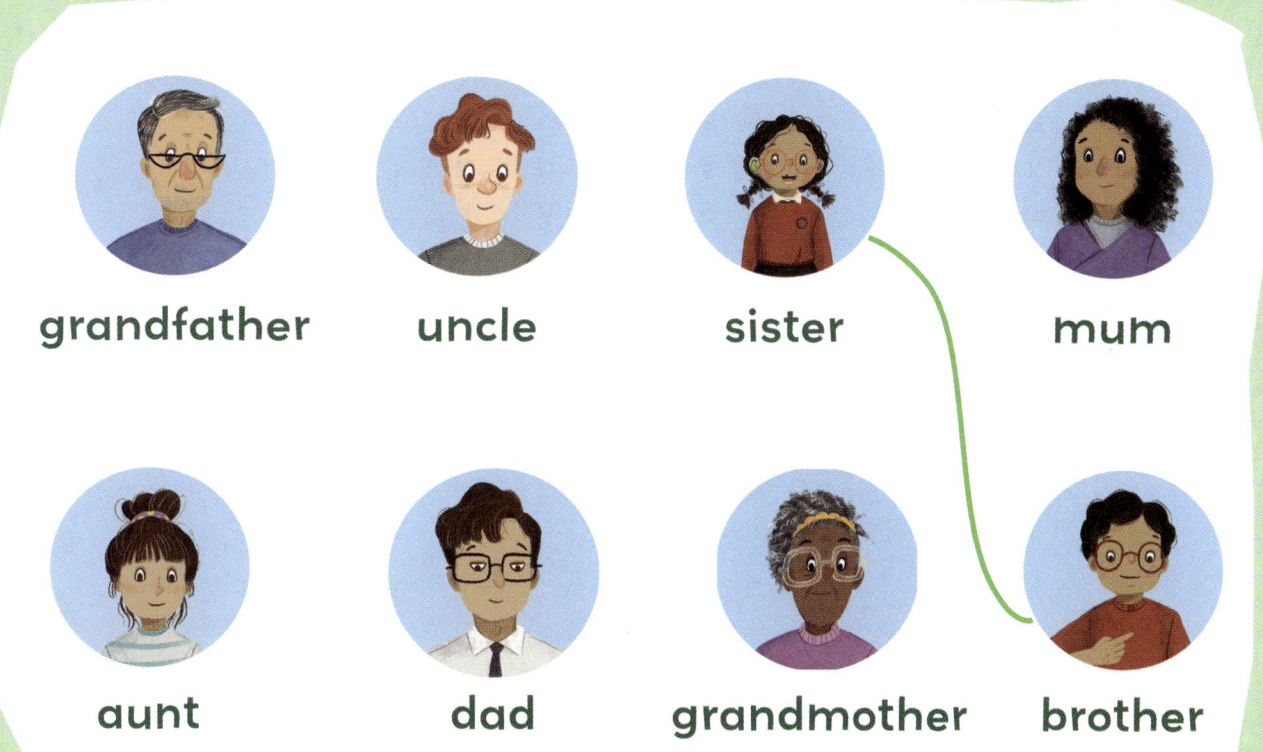

grandfather   uncle   sister   mum

aunt   dad   grandmother   brother

Days of the week

Sort it!

Help Chester the robot put the days of the week in the correct order.

Uh oh!

Wednesday _____ Monday

Saturday _____

Friday _____

~~Monday~~ _____

Thursday _____

Tuesday _____

Sunday _____

Wordsearch

Can you find and write SIX days of the week in the wordsearch?

w	f	r	i	o	t	m	p	s
m	d	a	f	m	u	o	n	t
o	a	e	s	z	e	t	b	h
n	t	w	y	a	s	j	n	u
d	u	s	u	n	d	a	y	r
a	l	s	n	d	a	y	r	s
y	l	i	s	v	y	i	s	d
n	o	h	r	f	y	w	d	a
a	c	p	l	r	d	a	q	y
w	e	d	n	e	s	d	a	y
s	a	t	u	r	d	a	y	d

_____

_____

_____

_____

_____

_____

Picture clues

Use the picture clues to find Mia and Oscar's favourite days of the week. Write the first letter of each word. Example:

 star = s

Use the letters to find the day.

Mia's favourite day is _____ .

Oscar's favourite day is _____ .

Find the word

day
_____

week
_____

weekend
_____

Wordsquare

Cross out (x) any letter that is in the square more than one time. What is the word?

I	E	A
H	N	T
E	G	A

_____

Clue: It is when you are asleep.

Months of the year

Fill in the words

Write the letters to complete the names of the months.

J _ _ _ _ _ _

F _ _ _ _ _ _ _ _

M _ _ _ _ _

A _ _ _ _ _

M _ _ _

J _ _ _ _

J _ _ _

A _ _ _ _ _

S _ _ _ _ _ _ _ _

O _ _ _ _ _ _

N _ _ _ _ _ _ _

D _ _ _ _ _ _ _

My favourite month! Go online to write your favourite month on a calendar.

Circle the number

Count and (circle). How many months are there on Mia's calendar?

ten   eleven   twelve   thirteen

Did you know?

Ethiopia is in Africa. In Ethiopia, there are **13** months in a year. How many months are there in your year?

Which month is it?

This month does not have the letter **m** in it. It does have the letter **r** in it. It does have the letter **a** in it. It comes after **March**. Which month is it? _____

This month ends in the letter **r**. It does not have the letter **o** in it. It comes at **the end** of the UK year. Which month is it?

_____

This month has the same first letter as the name **Jane**. It has the same last letter as the month after **January**. It comes before a month with the first letter **A**. Which month is it?

_____

Time

Maze

Can you help Oscar find his way through the time maze? Say the times on the clocks as you go through the maze.

Bonus point

What time is in the middle of the maze?

Seasons

Trees

Draw and colour the tree for a season.
Circle the name of the season in your drawing.

spring

summer

autumn

winter

Bonus point
What season is it in
your country now?

Did you know?

We can divide the Earth into two parts called
hemispheres: the Northern hemisphere and
the Southern hemisphere.

The seasons in the Northern hemisphere are
the opposite of the seasons in the Southern
hemisphere. When it is summer in the
Northern hemisphere, it is winter in the Southern hemisphere.

Weather

Vowels

Write the vowels to make weather words.

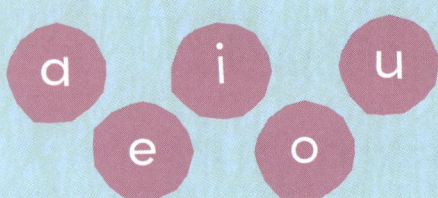

w ☐ ndy

f ☐ ggy

s ☐ nny

sn ☐ w ☐ ng

r ☐ ☐ n ☐ ng

cl ☐ ☐ dy

h ☐ t

☐ cy

st ☐ rmy

c ☐ ld

Word circles

Use each letter in the circle to make a weather word. Start with the letter in the middle of the circle.

Did you know?

There are about 2,000 storms on Earth every minute.

Crossword

Use the picture clues to complete the crossword with weather words.

Bonus point

What's the weather like today where you are?

It's _____.

↓ Down

1

2

4

6

8

→ Across

2

3

5

7

9

Prepositions of place

Find the word

What are the prepositions?

opposite _____

below _____

in _____

Picture puzzle

Write the words in this picture puzzle. Use the preposition in the blue squares to complete the sentence below the puzzle.
Clue: Look for where the ball is!

The ball is _____ the tree.

Draw a picture to show where the ball is.

Directions

Sort it!

Help Chester the robot put the directions in the correct order to get to school.

Uh oh!

☐ Go right.	☐ Go left.
☐ Go right.	☐ Go right.
☐ Go right.	☐ Go left.
☐ The school is on your left!	**1** Go straight on.

?

Did you know?

Birds always know which direction is north and which direction is south.

Numbers

Wordsearch

Can you find 18 numbers from 1–20 in the wordsearch?

1 ☐
2 ☐
3 ☐
4 ☐
5 ☐
6 ☐
7 ☐
8 ☐
9 ☐

```
b e l e v e n r j e v s l e f
o j t w b n r t h r e e j t i
e i g h t e e n d t m d o w v
t k x b j f g m n w n x n k e
e t o s e v e n y e i r p t t
e w d e a g w j t n n x n h y
n o c o h j m l v t e s i x l
s e v e n t e e n y l y o d t
f d t j h x o n e l a o v t e
e i g h t i l r m i e p b o n
o s g o x c h s i x t e e n b
t w e l v e p r x f i f b p y
u t w n i n e t e e n r e f i
r i t h i r t e e n t h i w v
f o u r t e e n t a n m k p y
```

20 ☐
19 ☐
18 ☐
17 ☐
16 ☐

10 ☐   11 ☐   12 ☐   13 ☐   14 ☐   15 ☐

Bonus point

Write the words for the two numbers not in the wordsearch.

☐

Lots of words

What number words can you see?

fsoirxtty	_____
tweighty	_____
zéour	_____
ninlethirty	_____

What age are they?

How old is each person?

Anoushka is thirty + ten. How old is she?

She is _____.

Cosmo is four + two + one. How old is he?

He is _____.

Bip is forty + five + five + twenty. How old is he?

He is _____.

Shapes

Picture puzzle

Write the words in this picture puzzle to find Mia's favourite shape.

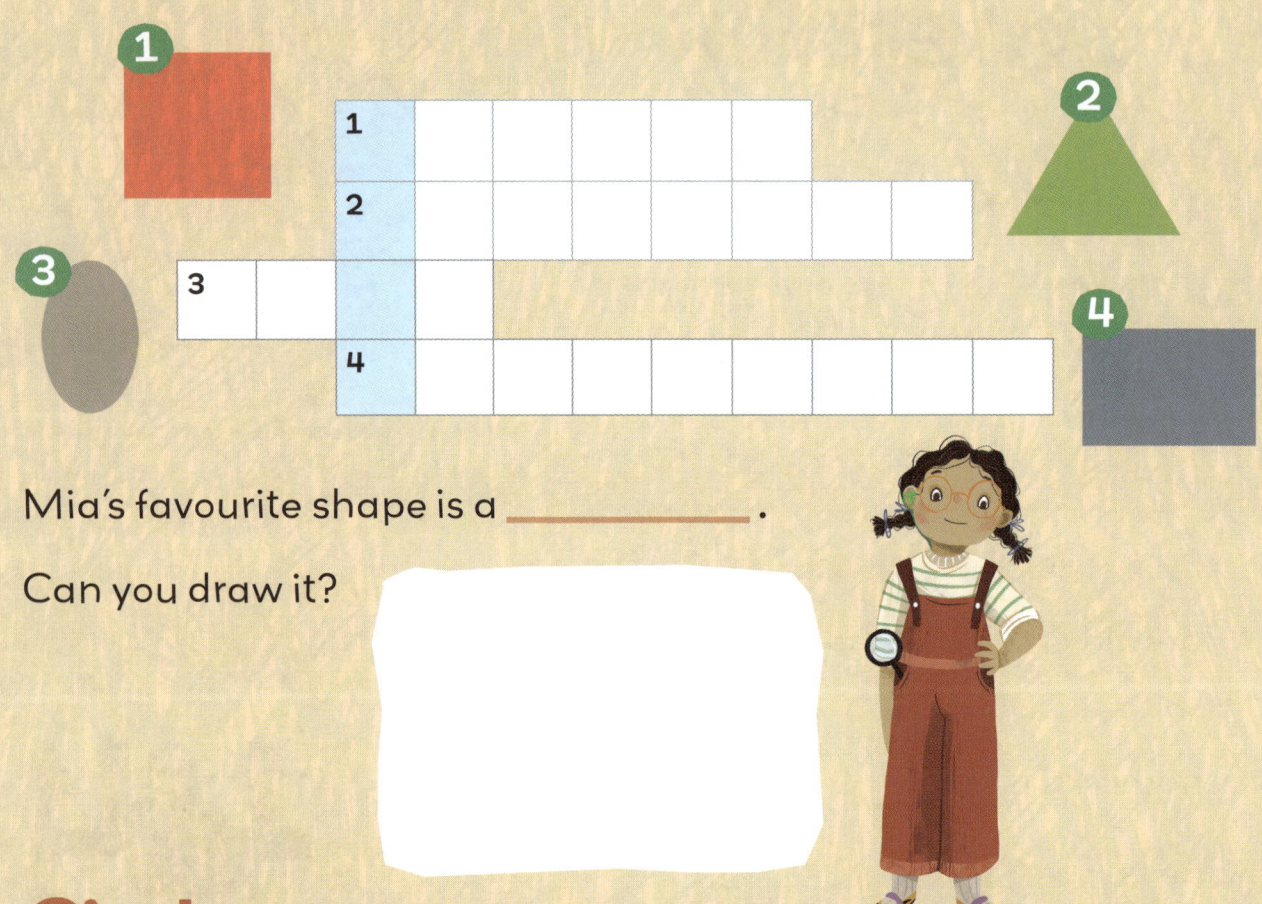

Mia's favourite shape is a _____ .

Can you draw it?

Circles

How many of these circle-shaped things can you find?

- [ ] a wheel
- [ ] a tennis ball
- [ ] a plate
- [ ] an orange
- [ ] a watermelon

School subjects

Follow the lines

Follow the lines and say the children's favourite school subjects.

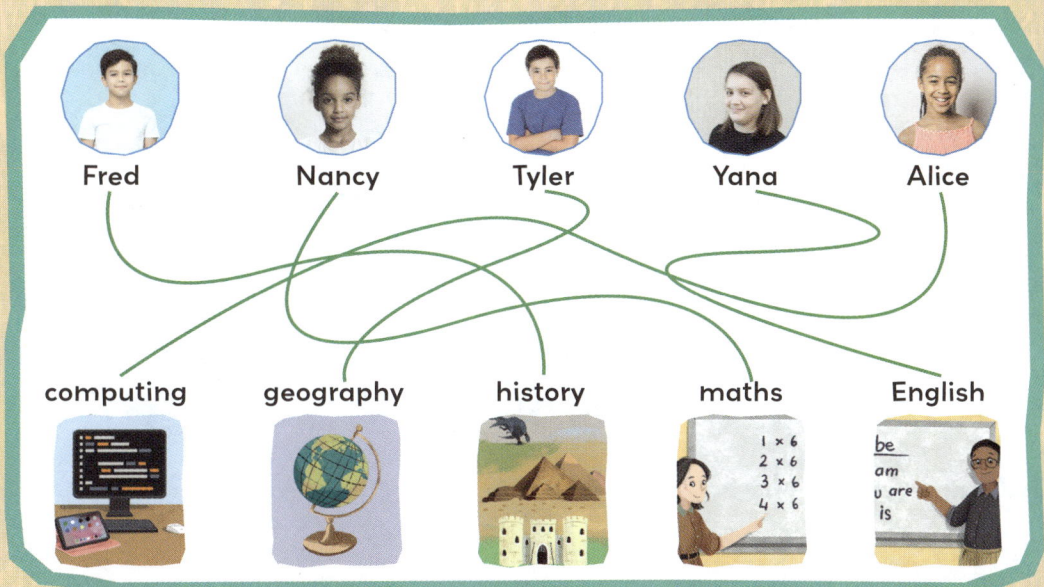

Fred Nancy Tyler Yana Alice

computing geography history maths English

Crack the code

Write the letter for each picture to find Oscar's favourite school subject.

= a
= c
= e
= h
= i
= k
= l
= n
= r
= s
= t

Fun with codes! Go online to have more fun with codes.

Bonus point

Write the word 'art' in code here.

Parts of the body

Photo scramble

What can you see? Use the letters to make words for parts of the body.

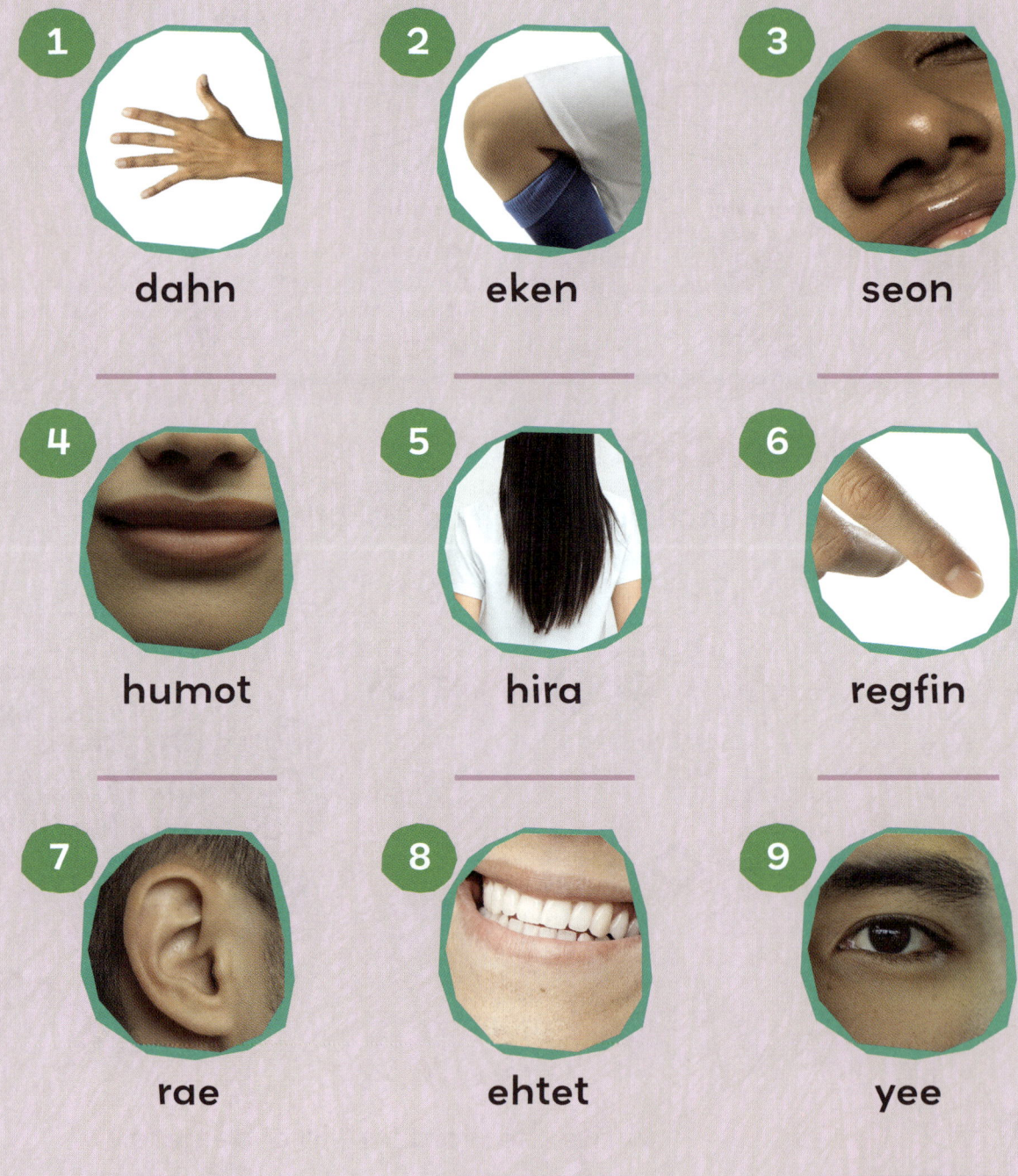

1 dahn

2 eken

3 seon

4 humot

5 hira

6 regfin

7 rae

8 ehtet

9 yee

True or false?

What do you know? Read and choose.

1 Children have twenty teeth.
True ☐   False ☐

2 Most spiders have eight eyes.
True ☐   False ☐

3 People can't have green eyes.
True ☐   False ☐

4 An elephant's nose is called a trunk.
True ☐   False ☐

5 Bees don't have knees.
True ☐   False ☐

6 Worms don't have eyes.
True ☐   False ☐

7 Sharks have the strongest teeth.
True ☐   False ☐

8 Polar bears don't have toes.
True ☐   False ☐

Bonus point

Write your own True or false? question about a part of the body.

_____

True ☐   False ☐

Answer: _____

Let's mix it up!

Odd one out

Find and cross out (x) the odd word out. Draw lines to match to the topic.

winter	su~~n~~ny	spring	summer

square	star	triangle	eye

July	Friday	Tuesday	Sunday

foggy	icy	midday	stormy

calendar	wife	sister	cousin

Weather

Days of the week

Seasons

Family

Shapes

Letter add

Add a letter or letters to the word on the left to make a new word on the right. Use the picture clues to help you.

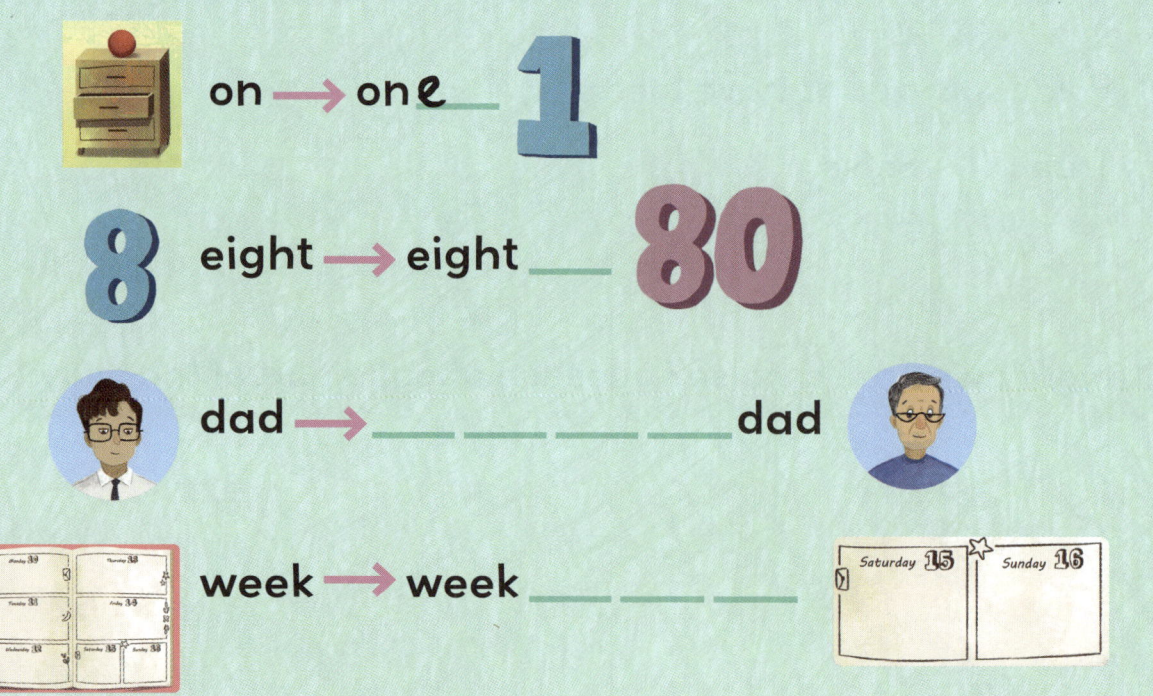

on → one ___ 1

8 eight → eight ___ 80

dad → ___ ___ ___ ___ dad

week → week ___ ___ ___ ___

Wordsquares

Cross out (x) any letter that is in the square more than one time. What is the word?

1

E	V	O
R	L	V
B	R	W

Clue: Not above.

_____

2

D	M	O
T	N	E
E	H	D

Clue: There are twelve in a year.

_____

3

E	B	P
T	T	S
B	A	H

Clue: A triangle is an example of this.

_____

Bonus point

Make your own wordsquare with a 5-letter word from this book.

Answer: _____

Let's play!

Let's get started board game

Play the game with your family or friends, you need 2–4 players.
Say the words in English.

Let's play!
Go online to
make your own
game spinner!

You need:

START

Good
luck!

1

2

3

4

17

16

15

14

18

19

20

21

22

How to play

- Start on the START square.
- Player 1. Spin the spinner.
- Count and move the number on the spinner.
- Name the thing in the picture. Each picture has a colour for the topic. Check the key!
- Player 2. It's your turn.
- The winner is the first player to get to the FINISH square. How many words did you know?

Key: | ■ Seasons | ■ Weather | ■ Time | ■ School subjects | ■ Shapes | ■ Numbers

FINISH
Well done!

Let's create and read!

Let's get started story

Use the clues to complete the story with your own words.

It is _____ . It is _____ . _____ and
       day of the week   month   family word

Mia are in the park. It is _____ .They walk. They go
                        weather

_____ . Mia counts the trees. There are _____ .
    direction   number

They go _____ . Mia sees a pretty leaf. It is _____
        direction   preposition of place

a big tree. Mia wants the leaf. She says, "Can I have

the leaf, please _____ ?" She puts the leaf in her
                 family word

bag. The time is _____ . It is time to go home.
                    time

Bonus point

Read your story out loud to your family and friends.

Let's write!

Let's get started kriss kross

Write all the words in the squares.
Use the number of letters to help you.

three letters
art
toe

four letters
aunt
east
head

five letters
April
March
north
right
south
sunny
teeth

six letters
August
cloudy

seven letters
English
parents
grandma

nine letters
computing

Answers

My family
Page 4
Maze

Word circles
cousin, father, uncle, mother

Page 5
Wordmatch
cousin, sister, grandma, uncle, brother, husband

Pairs
grandfather – grandmother, uncle– aunt, sister – brother, mum – dad

Days of the week
Page 6
Sort it!
Monday, Tuesday, Wednesday, Thursday, Friday, Saturday, Sunday

Wordsearch

w	f	r	i	o	t	m	p	s
m	d	a	f	m	u	o	n	t
o	a	e	s	z	e	t	b	h
n	t	w	y	a	s	j	n	u
d	u	s	u	n	d	a	y	r
a	l	s	n	d	a	y	r	s
y	l	i	s	v	y	i	s	d
n	o	h	r	f	y	w	d	a
a	c	p	l	r	d	a	q	y
w	e	d	n	e	s	d	a	y
s	a	t	u	r	d	a	y	

Bonus point ⭐
Friday is NOT in the wordsearch.

Page 7
Picture clues
Mia's favourite day is Sunday.
Sunday: star, umbrella, nine, dress, avocado, yellow
Oscar's favourite day is Thursday.
Thursday: tree, hat, umbrella, red, star, dress, avocado, yellow

Find the word
day, week, weekend

Wordsquare
night

Months of the year
Page 8
Fill in the words
January, February, March, April, May, June, July, August, September, October, November, December

Page 9
Circle the number
twelve

Which month is it?
April, December, July

Time
Page 10
Maze

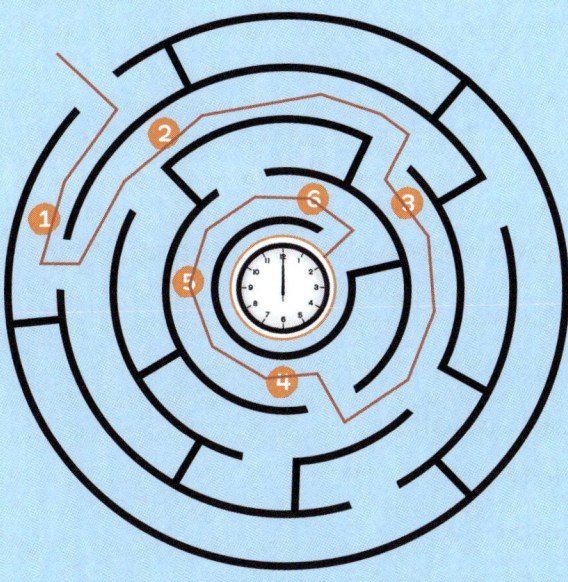

1. quarter past two, 2. one o'clock,
3. quarter to four, 4. eleven o'clock,
5. half past three, 6. seven o'clock

Bonus point ⭐

midday, midnight, twelve o'clock

Weather
Page 12
Vowels

windy, foggy, sunny, snowing,
raining, cloudy, hot, icy, stormy,
cold

Word circles

foggy, cloudy, windy, stormy

Page 13
Crossword

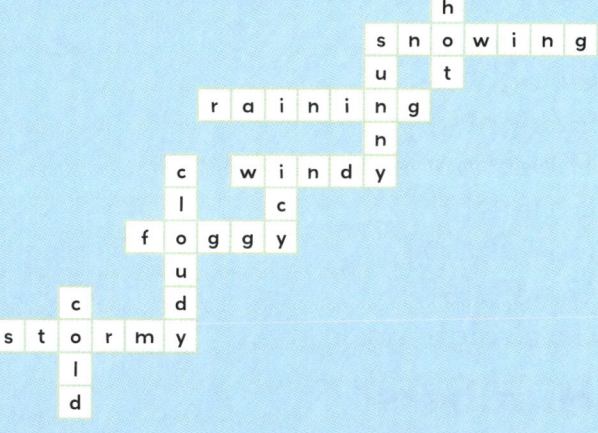

↓ Down

→ Across

Prepositions of place
Page 14
Find the word

opposite, below, in

Picture puzzle

The ball is **behind** the tree.

Directions
Page 15
Sort it!
Go right. [2]
Go right. [4]
Go right. [5]
The school is on your left! [8]
Go left. [3]
Go right. [7]
Go left. [6]
Go straight on. [1]

Numbers
Page 16
Wordsearch

b	e	l	e	v	e	n	r	j	e	v	s	l	e	f
o	j	t	w	b	n	r	t	h	r	e	e	j	t	i
e	i	g	h	t	e	e	n	d	t	m	d	o	w	v
t	k	x	b	j	f	g	m	n	w	n	x	n	k	e
e	t	o	s	e	v	e	n	y	e	i	r	p	t	t
e	w	d	e	a	g	w	j	t	n	n	x	n	h	y
n	o	c	o	h	j	m	l	v	t	e	s	i	x	l
s	e	v	e	n	t	e	e	n	y	l	y	o	d	t
f	d	t	j	h	x	o	n	e	l	a	o	v	t	e
e	i	g	h	t	i	l	r	m	i	e	p	b	o	n
o	s	g	o	x	c	h	s	i	x	t	e	e	n	o
t	w	e	l	v	e	p	r	x	f	i	f	b	p	y
u	t	w	n	i	n	e	t	e	e	n	r	e	f	i
r	i	t	h	i	r	t	e	e	n	t	h	i	w	v
f	o	u	r	t	e	e	n	t	a	n	m	k	p	y

Bonus point ⭐
four and fifteen

Page 17
Lots of words
forty and sixty, twenty and eighty, zero and four, ninety and thirty

What age are they?
40/forty, 7/seven, 70/seventy

Shapes
Page 18
Picture puzzle

		¹s	q	u	a	r	e		
		²t	r	i	a	n	g	l	e
³o	v	a	l						
		⁴r	e	c	t	a	n	g	l	e

Mia's favourite shape is a **star**.

Circles

a wheel	4
a tennis ball	5
a plate	6
an orange	5
a watermelon	1

School subjects
Page 19
Follow the lines
Fred's favourite school subject is history.
Nancy's favourite school subject is maths.
Tyler's favourite school subject is geography.
Yana's favourite school subject is English.
Alice's favourite school subject is computing.

Crack the code
He likes science.

Bonus point
➡ ⭐ 📖

The body

Page 20
Photo scramble
1. hand, 2. knee, 3. nose, 4. mouth,
5. hair, 6. finger, 7. ear, 8. teeth,
9. eye

Page 21
True or false?
1. True,
2. True,
3. False – some people have green eyes,
4. True,
5. False – bees do have knees,
6. True,
7. False – people's teeth are as strong as sharks' teeth,
8. False – polar bears have five toes on each foot

Let's mix it up!
Page 22
Odd one out
sunny – the other words are seasons
eye – the other words are shapes
July – the other words are days of the week
midday – the other words are weather
calendar – the other words are family

Letter add
on**e**, eight**y**, **gran**dad, week**end**

Page 23
Wordsquares
1. below, 2. month, 3. shape

Let's play!
Pages 24–25
Let's get started board game
1. three,
2. geography,
3. snowing,
4. rectangle,

5. half past twelve,
6. raining,
7. a hundred (100),
8. winter,
9. autumn,
10. triangle,
11. forty (40),
12. sunny,
13. seventeen (17),
14. stormy,
15. spring,
16. art,
17. twelve o'clock,
18. summer,
19. quarter to twelve,
20. star,
21. quarter past twelve,
22. PE,
23. foggy,
24. oval,
25. science,
26. zero (0)

Let's write!
Page 27
Let's get started kriss kross

Word list

Do you know all the words in this book? Tick them when you learn them! To check the meaning and hear the words, go to **collins1000englishwords.com**

- a hundred
- above
- April
- arm
- art
- asleep
- August
- aunt
- autumn
- avocado
- bag
- ball
- bee
- behind
- below
- between
- big
- body
- brother
- calendar
- circle
- clock
- cloudy
- cold
- computing
- [to] count
- cousin
- dad
- day
- December
- direction
- dress
- ear
- east
- eight
- eighteen
- eighty
- elephant
- eleven
- English
- eye
- father
- family

- February
- fifteen
- finger
- five
- foggy
- foot
- forty
- four
- fourteen
- Friday
- geography
- grandad
- grandfather
- grandma
- grandmother
- green
- hair
- half past
- hand
- hat
- head
- history
- hot
- husband
- icy
- in
- in front of
- January
- July
- June
- knee
- leaf
- left
- leg
- March
- maths
- May
- midday
- midnight
- minute
- Monday
- month
- mother
- mouth

- mum
- night
- nine
- nineteen
- ninety
- north
- nose
- November
- number
- o'clock
- October
- on
- one
- opposite
- orange
- oval
- parent
- park
- PE
- plate
- polar bear
- quarter past
- quarter to
- raining
- rectangle
- red
- right
- Saturday
- school
- science
- season
- September
- seven
- seventeen
- seventy
- shape
- shark
- sister
- six
- sixteen
- sixty
- snowing
- south
- spider

- spring
- square
- star
- stormy
- straight on
- strong
- subject
- summer
- Sunday
- sunny
- teeth
- ten
- tennis ball
- thirteen
- thirty
- three
- Thursday
- time
- toe
- tree
- triangle
- trunk
- Tuesday
- twelve
- twenty
- two
- umbrella
- uncle
- under
- [to] walk
- watermelon
- weather
- Wednesday
- week
- weekend
- wheel
- wife
- windy
- winter
- worm
- year
- yellow
- zero